Contents

What is a sunflower? 4
Spring 6
1–2 weeks 8
4–6 weeks 10
6–8 weeks 12
Summer 14
9–12 weeks 16
13 weeks 20
14 weeks 22
16 weeks 24
How we use sunflowers 26
Life cycle 28
Fact file 30
Glossary 31
More books to read 32
Index 32

Some words are shown in bold, **like this**. You can find out what they mean by looking in the glossary.

What is a sunflower?

A field of bright yellow sunflowers makes everyone smile!

Sunflowers are tall plants with large, flat flowers. They come from North America, but now they grow in other parts of the world, too.

LIFE CYCLE OF A...

Sunflower

Revised and Updated

Angela Royston

www.heinemannlibrary.co.uk
Visit our website to find out more information about Heinemann Library books.

To order:
Phone +44 (0) 1865 888066
Fax +44 (0) 1865 314091
Visit www.heinemannlibrary.co.uk

Heinemann Library is an imprint of Capstone Global Library Limited, a company incorporated in England and Wales having its registered office at 7 Pilgrim Street, London, EC4V 6LB - Registered company number: 6695582

"Heinemann" is a registered trademark of Pearson Education Limited, under licence to Capstone Global Library Limited

Second edition first published in hardback and paperback in 2009

Edited by Adrian Vigliano, Harriet Milles, and Diyan Leake
Designed by Kimberly R. Miracle and Tony Miracle
Original illustrations ©Capstone Global Library Limited 1998, 2009
Illustrated by Alan Fraser
Picture research by Tracy Cummins and Heather Mauldin
Originated by Chroma Graphics (Overseas) Pte. Ltd.
Printed in China by South China Printing Company Ltd.

ISBN 978 0431 99950 0 (hardback)
13 12 11 10 09
10 9 8 7 6 5 4 3 2 1

ISBN 978 0431 99968 5 (paperback)
13 12 11 10 09
10 9 8 7 6 5 4 3 2 1

British Library Cataloguing in Publication Data
Royston, Angela.
Life cycle of a sunflower. -- 2nd ed.
1. Sunflowers--Life cycles--Juvenile literature.
I. Title II. Sunflower
571.8'2399-dc22
A full catalogue record for this book is available from the British Library.

Acknowledgements
We would like to thank the following for permission to reproduce photographs: Getty Images pp. **4** (©Jim Cummins), **6** (©Dorling Kindersley), **27** (©Dorling Kindersley/Peter Anderson); Holt Studios International pp. **7**, **8**, **10**, **21**, **28 top left**, **28 top right** (©Nigel Cattlin); Photolibrary pp. **9**, **12**, **13**, **29 top left** (©OSF/Stephen Downer), **15** (©JTB Photo); Photoshot pp. **16** (©NHPA/A N T), **24** (©NHPA/Christophe Ratier); Shutterstock pp. **5**, **26** (©Antonio Jorge Nunes), **11**, **28 bottom** (©Sergiy Goruppa), **14** (©Levgeniia Tikhonova), **17** (©Krzysztof Slusarczyk), **18** (©Jasenka Luksa), **19**, **29 top right** (©Jiri Vaclavek), **20**, **22**, **29 bottom** (©Vladimir Mucibabic), **23** (©Sebastian Knight), **25** (©Slophoto).

Cover photograph of a sunflower reproduced with permission of Getty Images (©DAJ).

We would like to thank Michael Bright for his invaluable help in the preparation of this book.

Every effort has been made to contact copyright holders of material reproduced in this book. Any omissions will be rectified in subsequent printings if notice is given to the publisher.

There are several kinds of sunflowers of different sizes and colours. The sunflower in this book has bright yellow petals.

Yellow sunflowers look a bit like the Sun!

8 weeks

9-12 weeks

13-16 weeks

Spring

Inside each sunflower seed is a tiny plant waiting to grow.

The sunflower seed is planted in the ground in spring, when the soil is warm and damp.

The **roots** of the plant push down through the soil. They are covered in tiny hairs which take in water. A green shoot grows upwards.

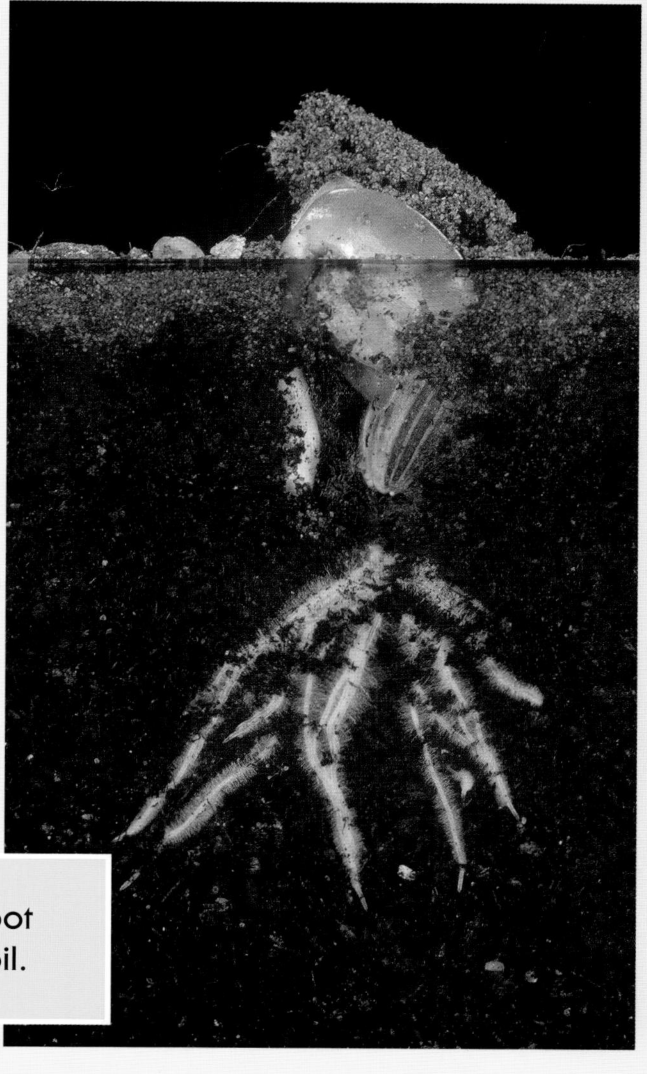

Here you can see the green shoot pushing upwards through the soil.

1–2 weeks

The first leaves open out. They use sunlight, air, and water to make food for the plant.

Now the green shoot has pushed right through the soil.

More leaves grow at the tip of the stem. The stem is covered with fine hairs. The hairs are to stop **insects** from climbing up the stem.

The plant grows taller and taller.

8 weeks

9-12 weeks

13-16 weeks

4–6 weeks

The leaves of the sunflower plant grow bigger.

Under the ground, the sunflower's **roots** grow longer. They take in the water and **minerals** the plant needs to stay alive and go on growing.

A large bud has formed at the top of the stem. It is protected by pointed green **bracts**. The bracts look like small leaves.

The bracts have sharp ends to protect the bud from animals, birds, and **insects**.

8 weeks

9-12 weeks

13-16 weeks

6–8 weeks

The **bracts** unfold and the bud begins to open.

The bud is nearly ready to open into a flower.

3 days

1 week

6 weeks

Underneath the bracts are lots of yellow petals.

Here you can see the yellow flower petals pushing out of the bud.

8 weeks

9-12 weeks

13-16 weeks

Summer

The plant keeps growing taller and taller. The flowers open out. Each **flower-head** contains many tiny flowers.

The petals open, and the flower-head grows bigger and wider.

Sunflowers need plenty of sunshine to help them grow.

The flower-heads face the Sun as it rises in the morning.

8 weeks

9-12 weeks

13-16 weeks

9–12 weeks

You can see the yellow pollen dust on the flower-head.

Each **flower-head** is made up of hundreds of tiny flowers called **florets**. The tips of these florets are covered with a fine yellow dust called **pollen**.

3 days

1 week

6 weeks

Bees like the sunflowers' bright yellow colour.

The flower-head is growing bigger. Bees see the bright yellow petals. They come to the flower-head to collect pollen.

8 weeks

9-12 weeks

13-16 weeks

As the bee crawls across the **florets**, the **pollen** sticks to its body and legs. Soon the bee is covered with pollen dust.

The bee flies from one **flower-head** to another.

The pollen rubs off the bee's body into the florets.

In the centre of each floret is a tiny egg called an **ovule**. When the pollen joins with the ovule it becomes a seed.

8 weeks

9-12 weeks

13-16 weeks

13 weeks

Soon the florets have no **pollen** left.

Inside each **floret** a seed is beginning to swell. The petals round the **flower-head** **wither** and fall off.

Now the petals have gone and only seeds are left.

The flower-heads become darker and turn almost black. Some are so heavy they droop from the end of the stems.

8 weeks

9-12 weeks

13-16 weeks

14 weeks

The sunflower's seeds are black and shiny.

The **florets wither** too. The **flower-head** is now a flat disk of seeds.

Birds like to feed on sunflower seeds.

The birds drop some of the seeds as they fly away. These may grow into new plants next year.

16 weeks

The farmer uses a big machine to harvest the sunflower seeds.

All the leaves have **withered** and died. The farmer has come to **harvest** the sunflower seeds. The harvester machine cuts the plants and shakes out the seeds.

3 days

1 week

6 weeks

The harvester missed this plant!

Some of the seeds fall to the ground. They will grow into new plants next spring.

How we use sunflowers

Farmers grow sunflowers especially for their seeds.

There is oil inside sunflower seeds. Some of the **harvested** seeds are squeezed and made into sunflower oil. The oil is used for cooking and eating.

Some seeds are crushed and made into animal feed. Some seeds are roasted for us to eat as snacks. Some pets like to eat sunflower seeds, too.

Some seeds are kept to be planted next spring.

8 weeks

9-12 weeks

13-16 weeks

Life cycle

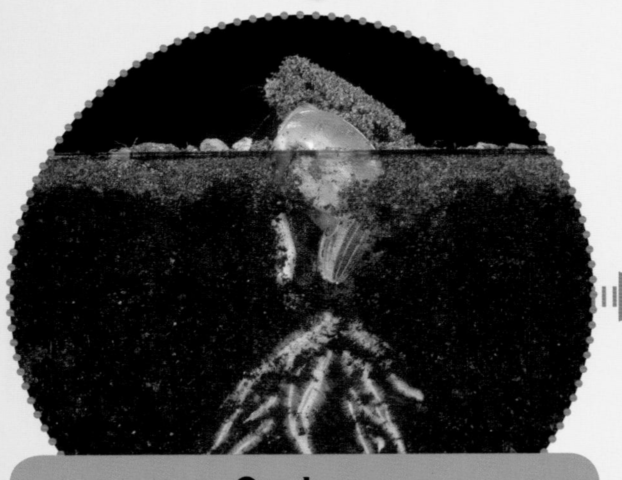

3 days

1 week

6 weeks

8 weeks

9–12 weeks

13–16 weeks

Fact file

- Sunflowers can grow to over 7 metres (23 feet) tall. That can be taller than a one-storey house.
- The sunflower's **flower-heads** can be 30–40 centimetres (12–15 inches) across – as big as a dinner plate.
- Each flower-head may produce 1,000 seeds. Most seeds are made into oil and margarine.
- Sunflowers grow all over the world. More are grown in Russia than in any other country.

Glossary

bracts parts of a plant that protect the bud while it grows. In most other kinds of flowers they are called sepals.

floret tiny flower, which is part of a flower-head

flower-head flower that is made up of many tiny florets

harvest gather in ripe crops

insect small animal that has six legs, a body with three main parts, and wings

minerals chemicals that the plant needs to stay healthy

ovule female egg that joins with male pollen to form a seed

pollen tiny male seeds of a plant

roots parts of a plant that grow under the ground and take in water

wither dry up; shrivel

More books to read

World of Plants: Why Do Plants Have Flowers?, Louise and Richard Spilsbury (Heinemann Library, 2005)

Investigate: Plants, Charlotte Guillain and Sue Barraclough (Heinemann Library, 2008)

Index

bracts 11, 12, 13
bud 11, 12
florets 16, 18, 19, 20, 22
flower-head 14, 15, 16, 17, 18, 20, 21, 22, 30
leaves 8, 9, 10, 11, 24
ovule 19
petals 5, 13, 14, 17, 20, 21
pollen 16, 17, 18, 19
roots 7, 10
seeds 6, 19, 20, 21, 22, 23, 24, 25, 26, 27, 30
shoot 7, 8
soil 6, 7, 8
stem 9, 11, 21